Lost.

by Gabby Pritchard

illustrated by Jon Stuart

 CAMBRIDGE
UNIVERSITY PRESS

 UCL
Institute of Education

One hot day, a cricket sat in the long grass.

He yawned.

'Time for a nap,' he said.

Soon he was snoring.

'Boo-hoo!'

The cricket opened an eye.

'Boo-hoo!'

'Who is crying?' said the cricket.

The cricket jumped over
the long grass.
He saw a big, green leaf.
It was shaking.

'BOO-HOO-HOO!'

'A talking leaf?' said the cricket.

A head peeped out from under the leaf.

BOOO-HOOO-HOOO!

7

'Hello,' said the cricket.
'Can I help you, little ant?'

A big tear rolled down
the ant's face.

'I'm lost!' said the ant.
'Please help me find my nest!'

'Jump on my back,'
said the cricket.

They jumped from nest to nest but they did not find the ant's home.

The cricket was very tired.

He jumped onto a tree.

'Let's rest here,' he said.

'That's my brother!'
shouted the ant.

'Where?' said the cricket.

The cricket looked down
and he saw a big nest.

A little ant was waving.

'Hold on!' said the cricket.

He jumped out of the tree ...

... and landed on top of
the ant's nest.

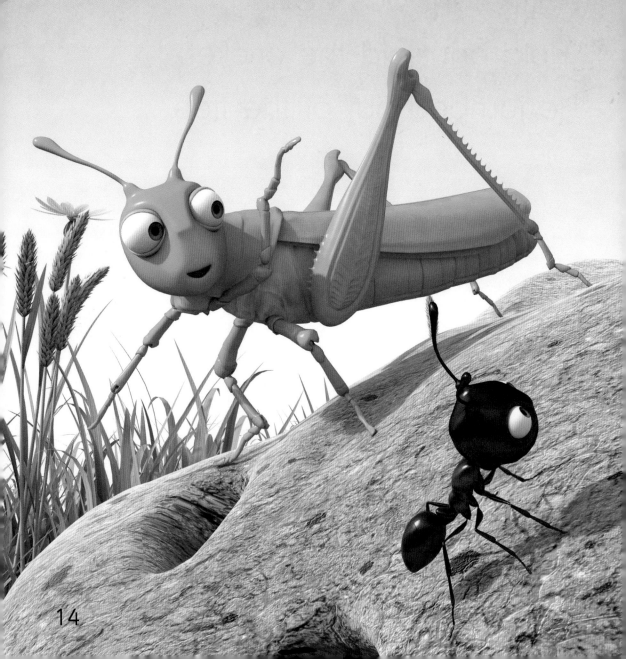

'Thank you for helping me find my home,' said the ant.

'You are welcome,' said the cricket.

Then he waved and went back into the long grass for a long nap!

Lost! 🐛 Gabby Pritchard

Teaching notes written by Sue Bodman and Glen Franklin

Using this book

Developing reading comprehension

In a story about helping, a tiny ant is lost and a cricket helps him to find his way home. A sequence of events occurs. Causal connections aid comprehension throughout the storyline, whilst pictures offer support without conveying the precise meaning (page 11, for example).

Grammar and sentence structure

- Longer sentences, including use of conjunctions ('*They jumped from nest to nest but they did not find the ant's home.*') and adjectival phrases ('*over the long grass*', '*under the leaf*').

- Dialogue is fully punctuated with question marks and exclamation marks used to support expressive reading and to emphasise character ('*Can I help you, little ant?*', '*That's my brother!*').

- Use of elision ('*I'm*', '*Let's*') mirrors natural speech patterns.

Word meaning and spelling

- Alternative spellings of the digraph /ee/ ('*tree*', '*leaf*' '*me*').

- Spelling of regular past tense verbs ('*jumped*', '*opened*') with /ed/ inflectional endings.

Curriculum links

Science – The story could provide a fictional backdrop for a study of mini-beasts. Research habitats of ants, using non-fiction texts and the internet.

PSHE – The cricket is a natural predator of ants, yet in this story he helps the ant find his way home. Read stories where people have helped others, such as the biblical story of the Good Samaritan.

Learning outcomes

Children can:

- read aloud with appropriate pace and emphasis, noting punctuation

- attend to print, meaning, and sentence structure flexibly to support automatic self-correction

- decode phonically regular words fast so that fluency of reading is maintained.

A guided reading lesson

Book Introduction

Ask children to tell you what they know about crickets and ants. Give each child a copy of the book. Read the title and the blurb with them. Ask, *Why do you think the story is called 'Lost!'?*

Orientation

Give a brief overview of the story, using the same verb tense as used in the book: *The cricket was having a nap in the long grass when a noise woke him up. It was a tiny ant crying because he was lost and couldn't find his way home. Do you think the cricket will help? Shall we see?*

Preparation

Page 2: Point out the word '*cricket*' and ask the children to look carefully and read slowly it. Discuss the word '*yawned*' which is not supported by the illustration. Ask: *Why might he be yawning?* (because it was hot or because he was tired, for example). Point out the word '*snoring*' on page 3, and check children's understanding.

Pages 4 and 5: Look at the word '*Boo-hoo*' repeated on these pages. Check the children know this is a way of representing crying, and practise saying it in a crying voice. Ask: *Who is crying? Yes, I think you are right – it's the ant! Let's look and see.*